EXPLORING OPPOSITES

Top and Bottom

by Joy Frisch-Schmoll

Consulting Editor: Gail Saunders-Smith, PhD

CAPSTONE PRESS
a capstone imprint

Pebble Plus is published by Capstone Press,
1710 Roe Crest Drive, North Mankato, Minnesota 56003
www.capstonepub.com

Library of Congress Cataloging-in-Publication Data
Frisch, Joy.
   Top and bottom / by Joy Frisch-Schmoll.
      p. cm. — (Pebble plus. Exploring opposites)
   Includes index.
   Summary: "Full-color photographs and simple text introduce the concepts of top and bottom"—Provided by publisher.
   ISBN 978-1-62065-116-2 (library binding)
   ISBN 978-1-62065-901-4 (paperback)
   ISBN 978-1-4765-2125-1 (eBook PDF)
1. Space perception—Juvenile literature. 2. Space perception in children—Juvenile literature. I. Title.
   BF469.F754 2013
   153.7'52—dc23   2012033225

Editorial Credits
Jill Kalz, editor; Ted Williams, designer; Wanda Winch, media researcher; Jennifer Walker, production specialist

Photo Credits
Capstone Studio: Karon Dubke, 15, 21; Courtesy of Kevin Yen, 11; Dreamstime: Laurentiu Iordache, 5; iStockphotos Inc.: erlobrown, 13; Shutterstock: ifong, 17, Ivonne Wierink, 19, Le Do, 7 (flower), M. Unal Ozmen, cover (bottom scoops), margouillat photo, cover (ice cream cone), Sari ONeal, 7 (horse), Standa Riha, 9

Note to Parents and Teachers

The Exploring Opposites set supports English language arts standards related to language development. This book describes and illustrates the concepts of top and bottom. The images support early readers in understanding the text. The repetition of words and phrases helps early readers learn new words. This book also introduces early readers to subject-specific vocabulary words, which are defined in the Glossary section. Early readers may need assistance to read some words and to use the Table of Contents, Glossary, Read More, Internet Sites, and Index sections of the book.

Printed in the United States of America in North Mankato, Minnesota.
092012   006933CGS13

Table of Contents

What They Mean

Ride to the top,

and see like a bird.

"Top" is the highest part

of an object. "Bottom" is

the lowest. They're opposites.

What's on the Top?

The horse wears a hat

on the top of its head.

The hat has a flower

on the top.

A goat stands at the top
of the mountain.

See the horns on the top
of its head?

What's at the Bottom?

The puppy rests

at the bottom

of the stairs.

It's too small

to climb.

Luis plays outside

without shoes.

The bottoms of his feet

get dirty.

Top and Bottom

Jinks the cat sits

on the top.

Brandon lies

on the bottom.

Hungry for ice cream?

The scoop of chocolate

is on the top.

The scoop of vanilla

is on the bottom.

17

You Try It: Top or Bottom?

The biggest box is

on the _____

of the pile. The bow

is on the _____.

The ladders are

on the _____

of the truck.

The wheels are

on the _____.

Glossary

horn—a hard, bony growth on the heads of some animals

mountain—a very tall hill

object—anything that can be seen and touched; a thing

opposite—as different as possible

scoop—the amount held by a scoop, a tool shaped like a small shovel

Read More

Ayres, Katherine. *Up, Down, & Around.* Cambridge, Mass.: Candlewick Press, 2007.

Behrens, Janice. *Let's Find Rain Forest Animals: Up, Down, Around.* Let's Find Out Early Learning Books. New York: Children's Press/Scholastic, 2007.

Schaefer, Lola M. *What's Up, What's Down?* New York: Greenwillow Books, 2002.

Internet Sites

FactHound offers a safe, fun way to find Internet sites related to this book. All of the sites on FactHound have been researched by our staff.

Here's all you do:

Visit *www.facthound.com*

Type in this code: 9781620651162

Index

Word Count: 118
Grade: 1
Early-Intervention Level: 13